STICKER ATLAS™
DINOSAURS
and
Prehistoric Animals

Dear Parents:

This book is designed as an introduction to dinosaurs. We recommend that you learn about these ancient animals along with your children.

Our knowledge of dinosaurs is based upon skeletal remains and fossils discovered all over the world. Much of what we know is derived from scientific evidence but some knowledge is based on speculation of what scientists believe to be true.

Dinosaurs died out suddenly 65 million years ago. No one is certain as to why this happened.

As new and exciting discoveries are made, we will gain a better understanding of our past and the animals that roamed the earth millions of years ago. New theories and information will alter our opinions as scientists strive to unlock the mystery of the dinosaurs.

Cover and Interior Art
MJ Studios Inc.
Written by Carol Z. Bloch
M.Ed. The Johns Hopkins University
B.A. The George Washington University

D1466402

ACANTHOPHOLIS
(AH-KAN-THOF-O-LISS)
"THORNBEARER"

EUROPE

INTERESTING FACTS:

The **Acanthopholis** was a plant-eating animal that was one of the smaller dinosaurs. Its back legs were longer than its front legs. Small armored plates covered its heavy body. Spikes stuck out from its neck and shoulders.

When It Lived
LATE CRETACEOUS

Size
17 FEET

Weight
2 TONS (4,000 POUNDS)

ALBERTOSAURUS
(AL-BER-TUH-SAWR-US)
"ALBERTA LIZARD"

WHERE IT WAS FOUND

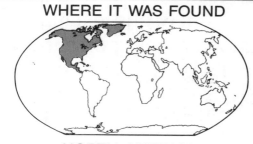

NORTH AMERICA

INTERESTING FACTS:

The **Albertosaurus** was a dangerous giant meat eater. With ferocious teeth in its huge head, it was able to kill its prey very quickly. This creature walked on its thick hind legs and had little use of its short front legs. Scientists have discovered many skeletons of this dinosaur in the United States.

When It Lived
LATE CRETACEOUS

Size
26 FEET

Weight
2 TONS (4,000 POUNDS)

ALLOSAURUS
(AL-UH-SAWR-US)

"DIFFERENT LIZARD"

INTERESTING FACTS:

The **Allosaurus** was a huge dinosaur with a tremendous head and a long, powerful tail. This meat eater's head had an unusual bony ridge that ran from its eyes to its snout. It had sharp teeth and could swallow its prey whole. Remains have been found all over the world.

When It Lived
LATE JURASSIC

Size
36 FEET

Weight
1-2 TONS (2,000-4,000 POUNDS)

ANCHICERATOPS
(AN-KEE-SER-A-TOPS)

"NEAR-HORNED FACE"

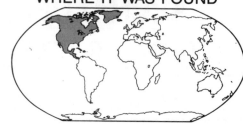
INTERESTING FACTS:

The plant-eating **Anchiceratops** had a small horn on its nose and two long horns above its eyes. A large, bony frill grew from its neck to its shoulders. This frill was different than those on other frilled dinosaurs which may have helped these animals recognize each other.

When It Lived
LATE CRETACEOUS

Size
19 FEET

Weight
7 TONS (14,000 POUNDS)

APATOSAURUS
(AH-PAT-UH-SAWR-US)
"DECEPTIVE LIZARD"

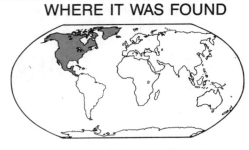

NORTH AMERICA

INTERESTING FACTS:

The **Apatosaurus** was a giant dinosaur that used to be known as **Brontosaurus.** It had a heavy body, thick legs and a very long neck and tail. It was a slow-moving, four-legged plant eater that ate an enormous amount of food. Though large in size, this giant had a small brain.

When It Lived
LATE JURASSIC

Size
75 FEET

Weight
33 TONS (66,000 POUNDS)

ARCHAEOPTERYX
(AR-KEE-OP-TER-IX)
"ANCIENT WING"

WHERE IT WAS FOUND

EUROPE

INTERESTING FACTS:

The **Archaeopteryx** may have been the world's first bird. It looked like a small dinosaur with feathers and wings. Three clawed fingers were found on the end of each wing. It couldn't fly very well and may have used its claws or its sharp teeth to catch fish.

When It Lived
LATE JURASSIC

Size
3 FEET

Weight
UNKNOWN

BRACHIOSAURUS
(BROCK-EE-O-SAWR-US)
"ARM LIZARD"

NORTH AMERICA AND AFRICA

INTERESTING FACTS:

The **Brachiosaurus** was one of the largest dinosaurs to roam the earth. Its thick front legs were longer than its back legs. It probably lived in herds in the wooded plains and ate leaves from treetops. It may have had two brains, one in its head and the other in its tail.

When It Lived
LATE JURASSIC

Size
74 FEET LONG
39 FEET HIGH

Weight
75 TONS (250,000 POUNDS)

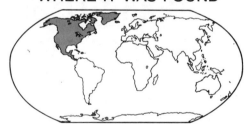

CAMPTOSAURUS
(KAMP-TUH-SAWR-US)
"BENT LIZARD"

WHERE IT WAS FOUND

NORTH AMERICA

INTERESTING FACTS:

The **Camptosaurus** had hooved feet that helped it quickly escape from an enemy. Although it was bent over, it could stand up straight and use its long tongue to gather leaves. It had a spike-shaped thumb on each hand.

When It Lived
**LATE JURASSIC TO
EARLY CRETACEOUS**

Size
4-23 FEET

Weight
UP TO 1,100 POUNDS

CARNOTAURUS
(KAR-NO-TAWR-US)

"MEAT-EATING BULL"

WHERE IT WAS FOUND

SOUTH AMERICA

INTERESTING FACTS:

The **Carnotaurus** was a vicious meat-eating dinosaur. It had a short snout with two large horns over its eyes. Its skin was rough and pebbly which was unusual for a meat eater.

When It Lived
LATE CRETACEOUS

Size
40 FEET

Weight
UNKNOWN

CERATOSAURUS
(SAIR-AT-O-SAWR-US)

"HORNED LIZARD"

WHERE IT WAS FOUND

NORTH AMERICA

INTERESTING FACTS:

The **Ceratosaurus** was a fierce meat eater with very sharp teeth. It had an unusual blade-like horn on its nose and small, bony plates down the middle of its back. This savage hunter probably stalked its prey in packs.

When It Lived
LATE JURASSIC

Size
20 FEET

Weight
1 TON (2,000 POUNDS)

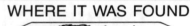

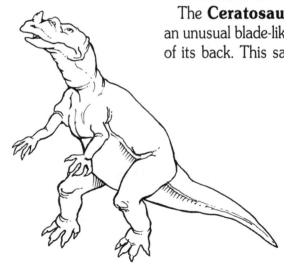

COELOPHYSIS
(SEE-LO-FISE-ISS)

"HOLLOW FARM"

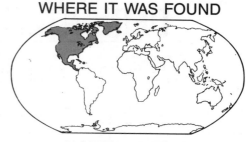
INTERESTING FACTS:

The **Coelophysis** was one of the first dinosaurs on earth. It was a very fast-running dinosaur. The **Coelophysis** looked very much like a lizard with a long, snaky neck and was the size of a large dog. It ran on its back legs and used the sharp claws on each hand to catch small animals.

When It Lived
LATE TRIASSIC

Size
10 FEET

Weight
65 POUNDS

DASPLETOSAURUS
(DASS-PLEE-TUH-SAWR-US)

"FRIGHTFUL LIZARD"

INTERESTING FACTS:

The **Daspletosaurus** was a relative of the Tyrannosaurus but was smaller and faster. It had a powerful head with huge jaws and lots of sharp teeth. Its front arms were small and weak and each had only two fingers. This savage hunter attacked and ate other dinosaurs.

When It Lived
LATE CRETACEOUS

Size
28 FEET

Weight
4 TONS (8,000 POUNDS)

DEINONYCHUS
(DINE-O-NYE-KUS)

"TERRIBLE CLAW AND OPPOSING HANDS"

WHERE IT WAS FOUND

NORTH AMERICA

INTERESTING FACTS:

The **Deinonychus** was a very powerful meat eater that would hunt in packs for animals even larger than itself. It used its very long tail for balance while it used its huge claws and feet to kill its prey. Each foot had a sharp claw that could go in and out whenever it was needed. Although it was a small dinosaur, it had a large brain and was a quick and clever hunter.

When It Lived
EARLY CRETACEOUS

Weight
170 POUNDS

Size
11 FEET LONG
5 FEET HIGH

EDMONTOSAURUS
(ED-MON-TUH-SAWR-US)

"EDMONTON LIZARD"

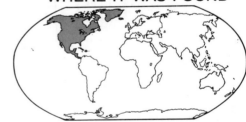

WHERE IT WAS FOUND

NORTH AMERICA

INTERESTING FACTS:

The **Edmontosaurus** was a large duck-billed dinosaur with a spoon-shaped beak. It walked on its hind legs and chewed tree leaves and pine needles with its hundreds of teeth. Some believe it had loose skin on the side of its nose that it blew up like a balloon to help it make a loud noise.

When It Lived
LATE CRETACEOUS

Size
33 FEET

Weight
3 TONS (6,000 POUNDS)

FABROSAURUS
(FAB-RUH-SAWR-US)
"FABRE'S LIZARD"

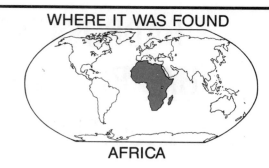

AFRICA

INTERESTING FACTS:

The **Fabrosaurus** was an early dinosaur that was smaller than man. Its hind legs were very strong which enabled it to run very fast from nearby enemies. Rows of strong, ridged teeth lined its jaws, so it could grind roots and other vegetation.

When It Lived
LATE TRIASSIC/EARLY JURASSIC

Weight
40 POUNDS

Size
3 FEET

GERANOSAURUS
(JER-AN-O-SAWR-US)
"CRANE LIZARD"

WHERE IT WAS FOUND

AFRICA

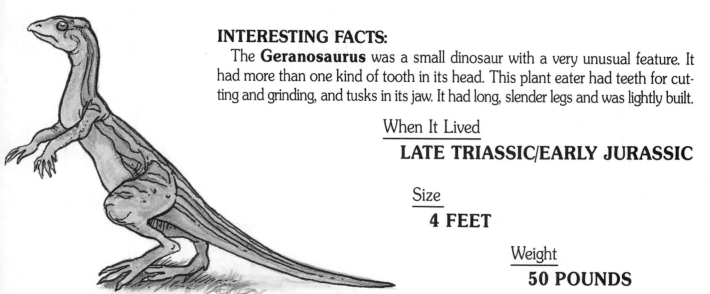

INTERESTING FACTS:

The **Geranosaurus** was a small dinosaur with a very unusual feature. It had more than one kind of tooth in its head. This plant eater had teeth for cutting and grinding, and tusks in its jaw. It had long, slender legs and was lightly built.

When It Lived
LATE TRIASSIC/EARLY JURASSIC

Size
4 FEET

Weight
50 POUNDS

HADROSAURUS
(HAD-RO-SAWR-US)

"BIG LIZARD"

NORTH AMERICA

INTERESTING FACTS:

The **Hadrosaurus** was the first dinosaur discovered in North America to be named. It is known as a duck-billed dinosaur because it had a beak similar to a duck. Humps sat on top of its flat head. This animal had hundreds of teeth it used to grind plants and roots.

When It Lived
LATE CRETACEOUS

Weight
3 TONS (6,000 POUNDS)

Size
26-32 FEET

HETERODONTOSAURUS
(HET-ER-UH-DON-TUH-SAWR-US)

"DIFFERENT-TOOTHED LIZARD"

WHERE IT WAS FOUND

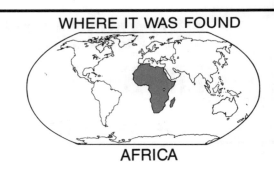

AFRICA

INTERESTING FACTS:

The **Heterodontosaurus** had three different types of teeth. It used its front teeth for cutting, molars for grinding, and had fangs on its lower jaw. Each foot had a claw at the back of its heel. This plant-eating dinosaur was able to run quickly to escape its enemies.

When It Lived
LATE TRIASSIC/EARLY JURASSIC

Weight
50 POUNDS

Size
4 FEET

HOMALOCEPHALE
(HO-MAH-LUH-SEF-UH-LEE)
"EVEN HEAD"

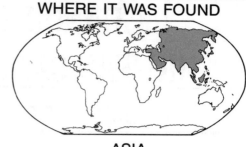

INTERESTING FACTS:

The **Homalocephale** had a very thick skull with several bumps on the top of its head. It walked on its back legs and used its tail to help keep its balance. This dinosaur may have been about the size of a very large goat and ate mostly plants.

When It Lived
LATE CRETACEOUS

Size
10 FEET

Weight
200 POUNDS

HYLAEOSAURUS
(HY-LAY-EE-UH-SAWR-US)
"WOOD LIZARD"

INTERESTING FACTS:

The **Hylaeosaurus** was shaped like a barrel and had an armored plating on its body. It had spikes and spines sticking out of the armor which protected it from other dinosaurs. Because it had small teeth, it was a plant eater.

When It Lived
EARLY CRETACEOUS

Size
20 FEET

Weight
UNKNOWN

IGUANODON
(IG-WAN-OH-DON)

"IGUANA TOOTH"

EUROPE, AFRICA, NORTH AMERICA, ASIA

INTERESTING FACTS:

In 1825, this creature became the second dinosaur to be named. It was named **Iguanodon** because its teeth resembled those of an iguana. Its spiked thumb helped protect it against its enemies and may have been used to pull down branches to eat.

When It Lived
EARLY CRETACEOUS

Size
29 FEET

Weight
5 TONS (10,000 POUNDS)

INDOSUCHUS
(IN-DOH-SOOK-US)

"INDIAN CROCODILE"

WHERE IT WAS FOUND

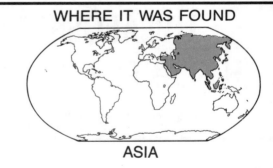

ASIA

INTERESTING FACTS:

Despite its name, the **Indosuchus** had nothing to do with crocodiles. It was related to a Tyrannosaurus but its size was smaller. It had fewer and smaller teeth than its relative. This meat eater walked on its hind legs and had little use for its front legs.

When It Lived
LATE CRETACEOUS

Weight
4 TONS (8,000 POUNDS)

Size
30 FEET

KRITOSAURUS
(KRIT-UH-SAWR-US)

"NOBLE LIZARD"

NORTH AMERICA

INTERESTING FACTS:

The **Kritosaurus** had a broad head with a hump on its nose. Webbed feet probably enabled it to swim. It walked through forests on its hind legs searching for plants to eat. Some scientists feel this may be a very close relative of the Hadrosaurus.

When It Lived
LATE CRETACEOUS

Size
30 FEET

Weight
3 TONS (6,000 POUNDS)

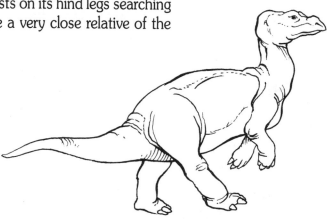

LAMBEOSAURUS
(LAM-BE-UH-SAWR-US)

"LAMBE'S LIZARD"

WHERE IT WAS FOUND

NORTH AMERICA

INTERESTING FACTS:

The **Lambeosaurus** was a duck-billed dinosaur with a broad beak. Plants were its main food. It had a large, unusually shaped crest on its head. It stood tall on its hind legs and had leathery skin. The **Lambeosaurus** had a very long tail.

When It Lived
LATE CRETACEOUS

Weight
2-5 TONS (4,000 TO 10,000 POUNDS)

Size
49 FEET

LESOTHOSAURUS
(LEH-SOTH-UH-SAWR-US)
"LESOTHO LIZARD"

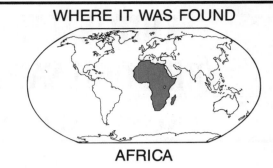

AFRICA

INTERESTING FACTS:

The **Lesothosaurus** was a small dinosaur about the size of a large dog. Small teeth lined the beak-like jaw in its little head. It probably ate plants when it was on all fours, but escaped danger by running swiftly on its two hind legs.

When It Lived
LATE TRIASSIC/EARLY JURASSIC

Size
3 FEET

Weight
40 POUNDS

LEXOVISAURUS
(LEX-OH-VUH-SAWR-US)
"LEXOVI LIZARD"

WHERE IT WAS FOUND

EUROPE

INTERESTING FACTS:

The **Lexovisaurus** had plates on its neck and back, and spines on its tail. Large spines stuck out sideways from its hips. This armor probably protected the animal from enemies. Plants made up its diet which it chewed with small teeth.

When It Lived
MIDDLE JURASSIC

Size
17 FEET

Weight
1 TON (2,000 POUNDS)

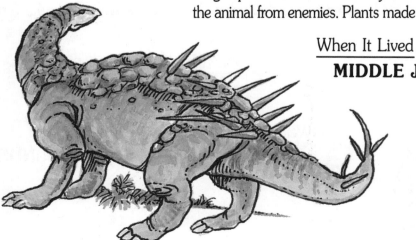

MAIASAURA
(MAH-EE-AH-SAWR-UH)
"GOOD MOTHER LIZARD"

NORTH AMERICA

INTERESTING FACTS:

The **Maiasaura** was given its name "Good Mother Lizard" because skeletons were found near nests of eggs and with babies. Each nest was seven feet across and two feet deep. After hatching, the young dinosaurs probably stayed close to home. The mother may have cared for her young and probably brought them food.

When It Lived
LATE CRETACEOUS

Size
30 FEET

Weight
2 TONS (4,000 POUNDS)

MASSOSPONDYLUS
(MASS-O-SPON-DIH-LUS)
"BULKY SPINY BONE"

WHERE IT WAS FOUND

AFRICA

INTERESTING FACTS:

The **Massospondylus** was a very common early dinosaur. It had powerful hind legs and strong arms. Each hand had a huge thumb with a large, curved claw. This dinosaur may have eaten both meat and plants. Pebbles in its stomach probably helped grind up plants so they could be digested more easily.

When It Lived
LATE TRIASSIC/EARLY JURASSIC

Weight
1,200 POUNDS

Size
13 FEET

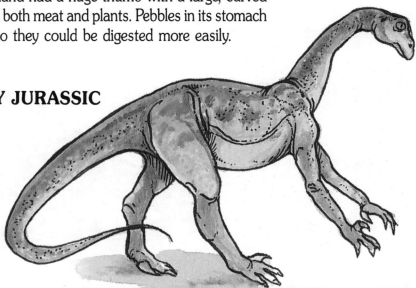

MEGALOSAURUS
(MEG-UH-LO-SAWR-US)
"BIG LIZARD"

EUROPE

INTERESTING FACTS:

The **Megalosaurus** was a meat-eating dinosaur with very long claws on its toes and hands. It had huge fangs and knife-like teeth. It walked on its huge hind legs. The **Megalosaurus** was the first dinosaur discovered and named.

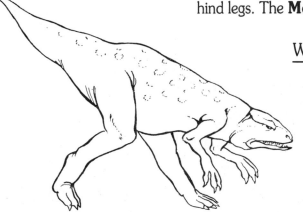

When It Lived

EARLY JURASSIC TO EARLY CRETACEOUS

Weight

1 TON (2,000 POUNDS)

Size

30 FEET

MELANOROSAURUS
(MEL-AN-OR-UH-SAWR-US)
"BLACK MOUNTAIN LIZARD"

WHERE IT WAS FOUND

AFRICA

INTERESTING FACTS:

The **Melanorosaurus** was the largest early dinosaur. Few enemies were able to attack it because of its huge size. This plant eater walked on all fours and had very heavy legs like an elephant. Its neck and tail were extremely long and heavy bones supported its huge body.

When It Lived

LATE TRIASSIC/EARLY JURASSIC

Weight

2 TONS (4,000 POUNDS)

Size

40 FEET

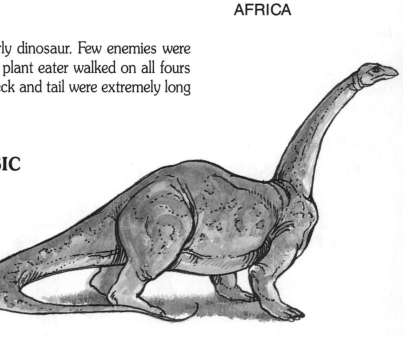

MONOCLONIUS
(MON-UH-CLO-NEE-US)
"SINGLE STEM"

NORTH AMERICA

INTERESTING FACTS:

The **Monoclonius** had a single, long horn growing on its nose and small bumps above its eyes. It had a short neck frill made of bone with two large holes in the frill. Scaly skin covered its body and its toes were hoofed. Its huge head stayed close to the ground where it grazed on plants.

When It Lived
LATE CRETACEOUS

Size
18 FEET

Weight
UNKNOWN

NODOSAURUS
(NO-DO-SAWR-US)
"KNOBBY LIZARD"

WHERE IT WAS FOUND

NORTH AMERICA

INTERESTING FACTS:

The **Nodosaurus** was covered with large and small armor-like plates. These plates made it difficult for other animals to attack this medium-sized dinosaur. Its tail dragged along the ground as it searched for soft plants to eat.

When It Lived
LATE CRETACEOUS

Size
18 FEET

Weight
2-3 TONS (4,000-6,000 POUNDS)

ORNITHOMIMUS
(OR-NITH-UH-MY-MUS)
"BIRD IMITATOR"

NORTH AMERICA, ASIA

INTERESTING FACTS:

The **Ornithomimus** looked like an ostrich without feathers. It was lightly built, therefore, it could outrun any other animal. Its mouth contained no teeth so its beak probably broke up the insects, fruit and small animals which it ate. Because it had a large brain, it is believed to be one of the most intelligent dinosaurs.

When It Lived
LATE CRETACEOUS

Weight
220 POUNDS

Size
11 FEET

OURANOSAURUS
(OUR-AHN-UH-SAWR-US)
"BRAVE MONITOR LIZARD"

WHERE IT WAS FOUND

AFRICA

INTERESTING FACTS:

The **Ouranosaurus** was a plant-eating dinosaur with very high spines running down its back and tail. These spines formed a kind of thin sail and may have acted as a solar panel to warm the animal. The **Ouranosaurus** could walk on all fours or its hind legs.

When It Lived
EARLY CRETACEOUS

Weight
4 TONS (8,000 POUNDS)

Size
23 FEET

OVIRAPTOR
(O-VEE-RAP-TOR)

"EGG THIEF"

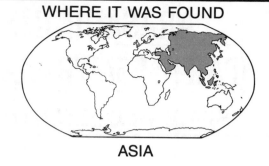

ASIA

INTERESTING FACTS:

The **Oviraptor** was a small dinosaur without teeth. It had a powerful beak that was able to crush bones and shells. This bird-like creature had large claws and long fingers it used to grasp its prey. It walked on two thin legs.

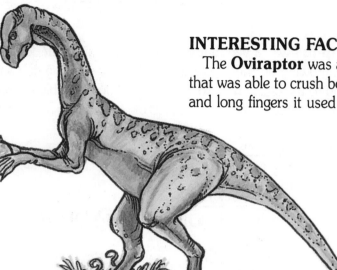

When It Lived
LATE CRETACEOUS

Weight
60 POUNDS

Size
6 FEET

PACHYCEPHALOSAURUS
(PAK-EE-SEF-UH-LO-SAWR-US)

"THICK-HEADED LIZARD"

WHERE IT WAS FOUND

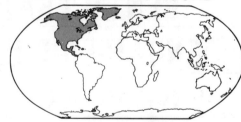

NORTH AMERICA

INTERESTING FACTS:

The **Pachycephalosaurus** was a large dinosaur with a nine inch plate of bone covering its brain. It used its domed head as a weapon against enemies. This plant eater's tail was stiff and may have been used to help the dinosaur keep its balance.

When It Lived
LATE CRETACEOUS

Size
17 FEET

Weight
450 POUNDS

PARASAUROLOPHUS
(PAR-AH-SAWR-OL-UH-FUS)
"SIMILAR CRESTED LIZARD"

NORTH AMERICA

INTERESTING FACTS:

The **Parasaurolophus** was a very unusual duck-billed dinosaur. It had a tube-like hollow crest growing on the top of its head and extending outward. Breathing tubes ran up to the crest and into the mouth. This probably enabled it to make a sound like a trombone. Its diet consisted of pine needles and leaves.

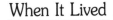

When It Lived
LATE CRETACEOUS

Weight
3 TONS (6,000 POUNDS)

Size
33 FEET

PENTACERATOPS
(PEN-TAH-SAIR-UH-TOPS)
"FIVE HORNED FACE"

WHERE IT WAS FOUND
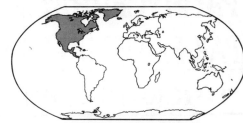
NORTH AMERICA

INTERESTING FACTS:

The **Pentaceratops** had more horns on its head than any horned dinosaur. It had a short nose horn, one above each eyebrow, and a smaller one on each cheek. This plant-eating dinosaur's neck frill was very long and may have been used to scare off enemies.

When It Lived
LATE CRETACEOUS

Weight
2 TONS (4,000 POUNDS)

Size
20 FEET

PLATEOSAURUS
(PLAY-TEE-UH-SAWR-US)

"FLAT REPTILE"

INTERESTING FACTS:

The **Plateosaurus** was a large dinosaur with a very long neck and tail. It had many rows of triangular-shaped small teeth which helped it shred plants. It may have swallowed stones to help it grind up the plants in its stomach. The **Plateosaurus** may have roamed the earth in herds.

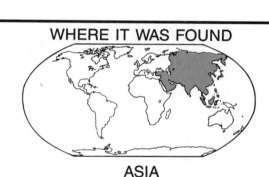

When It Lived
LATE TRIASSIC

Size
26 FEET LONG
15-20 FEET TALL WHEN
STANDING ON ITS HIND LEGS

Weight
UNKNOWN

PROTOCERATOPS
(PRO-TOE-SER-A-TOPS)

"FIRST HORNED FACE"

INTERESTING FACTS:

The **Protoceratops** was one of the first horned dinosaurs. It was a small dinosaur that did not have a true horn but had a bony bump on its head above a large beak. This plant-eating dinosaur had teeth for chopping instead of chewing. The first dinosaur egg ever found was from a **Protoceratops.**

When It Lived
LATE CRETACEOUS

Size
7 FEET LONG
30 INCHES HIGH

Weight
1.5 TONS OR 3,000 POUNDS

PTERODACTYLUS
(TER-UH-DAK-TUH-LUS)
"WING FINGER"

INTERESTING FACTS:

The **Pterodactylus** was a tiny bird-like creature with wings but may not have had any feathers. It had a long neck, face and hands. Its leg muscles controlled the movement of its wings. Insects and small crustaceans were probably its main food.

When It Lived
LATE JURASSIC

Size
2 FEET

Weight
UNKNOWN

QUETZALCOATLUS
(KET-SOL-KO-AT-LUS)
"FEATHERED SERPENT GOD"

INTERESTING FACTS:

The **Quetzalcoatlus** was the largest flying creature that ever lived. It may have been able to fly for hours at a time. Its long, slender beak may have been used to spear fish or to find other food.

When It Lived
LATE CRETACEOUS

Size
40 FOOT WINGSPAN

Weight
150 POUNDS

SAICHANIA
(SYE-CHAY-NEE-AH)
"BEAUTIFUL ONE"

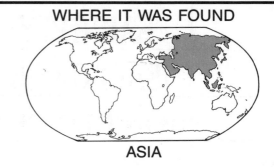
INTERESTING FACTS:

The **Saichania** was an armored dinosaur with its neck, back and stomach covered with bony plates and rows of spikes. Its tail had a bony club on the end of it. This club was probably used to attack flesh-eating dinosaurs. Many well-preserved skeletons of this plant eater have been found.

When It Lived
LATE CRETACEOUS

Weight
3-5 TONS (6,000-10,000 POUNDS)

Size
23 FEET

SALTASAURUS
(SALT-UH-SAWR-US)
"SALTA LIZARD"

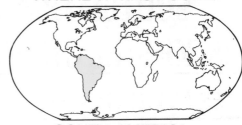

INTERESTING FACTS:

The **Saltasaurus** was a giant dinosaur with an elephant-like body. It could probably rear up on its hind legs to reach the highest branches of trees. This peaceful dinosaur had thousands of small armor plates all over its body for protection. It also used its long, thick tail to protect itself.

When It Lived
LATE CRETACEOUS

Weight
30 TONS (60,000 POUNDS)

Size
40 FEET

SALTOPUS
(SALT-O-PUS)

"LEAPING FOOT"

EUROPE

INTERESTING FACTS:

The **Saltopus** was a tiny, lightly built dinosaur which was able to run quickly from danger. It probably fed on insects and lizards. Its small hands had five fingers and could catch food. Standing only eight inches high, it was about the size of a cat.

When It Lived
LATE TRIASSIC

Weight
2 POUNDS

Size
2 FEET

SCUTELLOSAURUS
(SCOO-TEL-OH-SAWR-US)

"LITTLE SHIELD LIZARD"

WHERE IT WAS FOUND

NORTH AMERICA

INTERESTING FACTS:

The **Scutellosaurus** was a small plant eater with triangular-shaped teeth in a single row. Tiny, bony knobs protected its body. A tail longer than its entire body may have been used to help keep its balance. It had long back legs and short front legs and could probably run swiftly.

When It Lived
LATE TRIASSIC/EARLY JURASSIC

Weight
50 POUNDS

Size
4 FEET

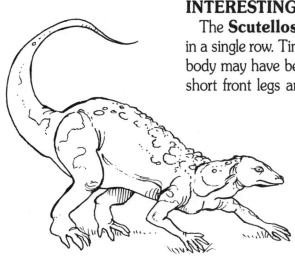

SEGISAURUS
(SEE-GIH-SAWR-US)

"SEGI LIZARD"

INTERESTING FACTS:

The **Segisaurus** was a small dinosaur about the size of a large rabbit or goose. It had slim hind legs that allowed it to run quickly from its enemies. It probably ate small lizards and insects.

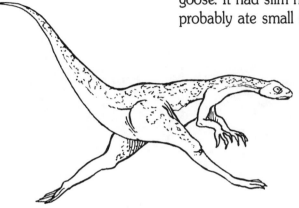

When It Lived
EARLY JURASSIC

Weight
20 POUNDS

Size
3 FEET

SEISMOSAURUS
(SYE-MO-SAWR-US)

"EARTHSHAKER LIZARD"

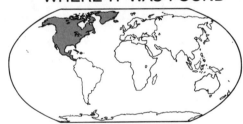

INTERESTING FACTS:

The **Seismosaurus** may have been the longest dinosaur that ever roamed the earth. It was recently discovered in 1984 and scientists are still excavating the site where it was found. It walked on all fours and probably had a very long tail.

When It Lived
LATE JURASSIC

Weight
80-100 TONS (160,000-200,000 POUNDS)

Size
120 FEET

SHANTUNGOSAURUS
(SHAN-TUNG-O-SAWR-US)
"SHANTUNG LIZARD"

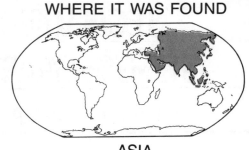

ASIA

INTERESTING FACTS:

The **Shantungosaurus** is the biggest duck-billed dinosaur ever discovered. Its head had a flat top and a flat beak. The front of this giant's mouth had no teeth so it chewed with its powerful jaw. It stored extra food in its cheeks to eat at a later time.

When It Lived
LATE CRETACEOUS

Weight
3-4 TONS (6,000-8,000 POUNDS)

Size
39-49 FEET

STAURIKOSAURUS
(STOR-IK-UH-SAWR-US)
"LIZARD OF THE SOUTHERN CROSS"

WHERE IT WAS FOUND

SOUTH AMERICA

INTERESTING FACTS:

Until recently, the **Staurikosaurus** was one of the oldest dinosaurs known. This meat-eating, small dinosaur probably had five fingered hands and five toed feet. It walked and ran very fast on two legs and had no known relatives.

When It Lived
MIDDLE TRIASSIC

Size
6 FEET 6 INCHES

Weight
65 POUNDS

STEGOSAURUS
(STEG-UH-SAWR-US)
"PLATED LIZARD"

NORTH AMERICA

INTERESTING FACTS:

The **Stegosaurus** is known for the big, bony plates on its neck and back. With its spiked tail, it defended itself against enemies. This scary-looking dinosaur had very small teeth and fed on plants and leaves.

When It Lived
LATE JURASSIC

Size
25 FEET

Weight
2 TONS (4,000 POUNDS)

STYRACOSAURUS
(STY-RAK-UH-SAWR-US)
"SPIKED LIZARD"

WHERE IT WAS FOUND

NORTH AMERICA

INTERESTING FACTS:

The **Styracosaurus** was a lizard with a short frill. It had one horn on its nose and six huge spikes attached to the back of its neck frill. Its nose horn was used to dig up roots and other plants to eat and to protect itself. It was a scary-looking dinosaur.

When It Lived
LATE CRETACEOUS

Weight
3 TONS (6,000 POUNDS)

Size
18 FEET

TRICERATOPS
(TRY-SAIR-UH-TOPS)

"THREE-HORNED FACE"

WHERE IT WAS FOUND
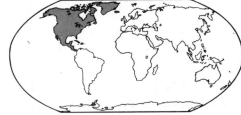
NORTH AMERICA

INTERESTING FACTS:

This very large and heavy dinosaur had a smooth, solid frill. It had a small nose horn and two very large horns on its head. The **Triceratops** was slow-moving and used these horns to protect itself. Scientists have identified five different species of this dinosaur from the many skeletons discovered.

When It Lived
LATE CRETACEOUS

Size
25 FEET

Weight
6 TONS (12,000 POUNDS)

TYRANNOSAURUS REX
(TIE-RAN-UH-SAWR-US)

"TYRANT LIZARD"

WHERE IT WAS FOUND

NORTH AMERICA

INTERESTING FACTS:

The **Tyrannosaurus Rex** was probably the most powerful and biggest meat eater that ever lived. It stood on huge back legs and had a very strong tail. Since it was hard for this large animal to move quickly, it waited until a smaller animal was close by to capture it for food. Its large head and body and dagger-like teeth made this dinosaur one of the most ferocious on earth.

When It Lived
CRETACEOUS PERIOD

Size
40 FEET LONG
18 FEET TALL

Weight
14,000 POUNDS

VELOCIRAPTOR
(VEH·LOSS·IH·RAP·TOR)
"SWIFT ROBBER"

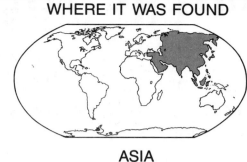

ASIA

INTERESTING FACTS:

The **Velociraptor** was a ferocious meat-eating dinosaur. It was small and agile and it could run quite fast. On the end of each of its three long fingers was a large claw it used to kill its prey. The velociraptor was about the size of a man.

When It Lived
LATE CRETACEOUS

Weight
UNKNOWN

Size
6 FEET

VULCANODON
(VUL·CAN·O·DON)
"VOLCANO TOOTH"

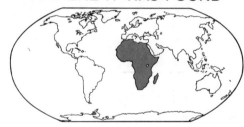

AFRICA

INTERESTING FACTS:

The **Vulcanodon** was a large plant eater with small, sharp teeth. It had thick elephant-like legs and a very long, sloped neck and tail. No skull has ever been found, so scientists have to guess at what its head may have looked like.

When It Lived
EARLY JURASSIC

Size
20 FEET

Weight
UNKNOWN

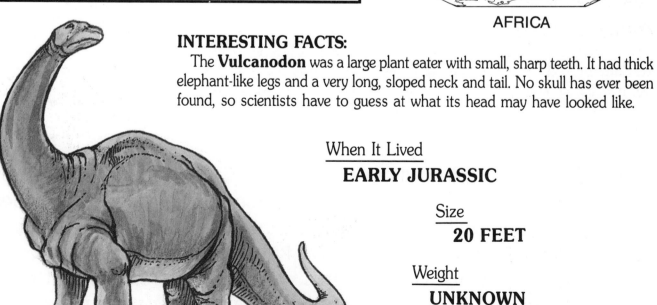

WHERE THEY LIVED...

Dinosaurs first appeared on Earth toward the end of the Triassic Period. They died out about 65 million years ago during the Cretaceous Period.

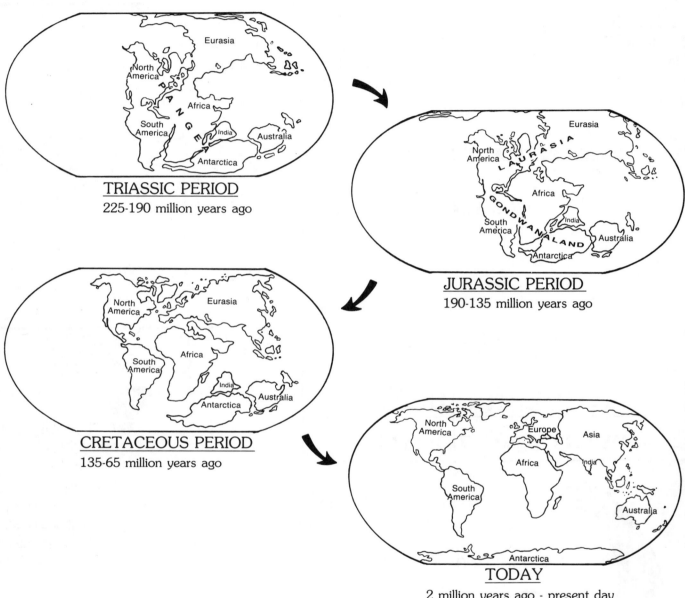

TRIASSIC PERIOD
225-190 million years ago

JURASSIC PERIOD
190-135 million years ago

CRETACEOUS PERIOD
135-65 million years ago

TODAY
2 million years ago - present day

Approximately 225 million years ago, all of the land masses on Earth were joined together. This one supercontinent was called Pangaea. It took millions of years for this huge land mass to break up and drift into the continents we know today. Millions of years from now the surface of the Earth will look different than it does today as the continental drift continues at a very slow pace.

WHEN THEY LIVED...

MESOZOIC ERA / *AGE OF REPTILES*

TRIASSIC PERIOD	JURASSIC PERIOD	CRETACEOUS PERIOD
Began 225 million years ago	Began 190 million years ago	Began 135 million years ago

STAURIKOSAURUS

SEGISAURUS
VULCANODON

DEINONYCHUS
HYLAEOSAURUS
IGUANODON
OURANOSAURUS

LEXOVISAURUS
MEGALOSAURUS

TYRANNOSAURUS REX

COELOPHYSIS
PLATEOSAURUS
SALTOPUS

ALLOSAURUS
APATOSAURUS
ARCHAEOPTERYX
BRACHIOSAURUS
CERATOSAURUS
PTERODACTYLUS
SEISMOSAURUS
STEGOSAURUS

ACANTHOPHOLIS
ALBERTOSAURUS
ANCHICERATOPS
CARNOTAURUS
DASPLETOSAURUS
EDMONTOSAURUS
HADROSAURUS
HOMALOCEPHALE

FABROSAURUS
GERANOSAURUS
HETERODONTOSAURUS
LESOTHOSAURUS
MASSOSPONDYLUS
MELANOROSAURUS
SCUTELLOSAURUS

CAMPTOSAURUS

INDOSUCHUS
KRITOSAURUS
LAMBEOSAURUS
MAIASAURA
MONOCLONIUS
NODOSAURUS
ORNITHOMIMUS
OVIRAPTOR
PACHYCEPHALOSAURUS
PARASAUROLOPHUS
PENTACERATOPS
PROTOCERATOPS
QUETZALCOATLUS
SAICHANIA
SALTASAURUS
SHANTUNGOSAURUS
STYRACOSAURUS
TRICERATOPS
VELOCIRAPTOR

Glossary of Terms

amphibians - cold-blooded animals with backbones that are able to live on land and in the water

birds - warm-blooded animals with backbones, feathers and wings

carnivore - meat-eating animal

cold-blooded - not able to regulate body temperature

Cretaceous Period - 135 to 65 million years ago

dinosaurs - extinct animals that roamed the earth until 65 million years ago, means "terrible lizard"

extinct - no longer existing

fangs - extra long, sharp teeth

fossils - remains of an animal or plant reserved in rock

herbivore - plant-eating animal

invertebrates - animals without backbones

Jurassic Period - 190 to 135 million years ago

mammals - warm-blooded animals with backbones, fur or hair that feed their young with milk from mammary glands

paleontology - the science of studying the past from geologic records and fossils

prehistoric - time before written language existed

reptiles - cold-blooded animals with backbones, usually covered with scales or horny plates

Tertiary Period - 65 million years ago to present

Triassic Period - 225 to 190 million years ago

vertebrates - animals with a backbone

warm-blooded - able to regulate body temperature